Confessions of a Shower Tapper

Confessions of a Shower Tapper

THE ULTIMATE GUIDE TO LIVING YOUR PURPOSE WITH EFT

Rev. Terri Ann Heiman

ISBN: 069242010X
ISBN 13: 9780692420102
Library of Congress Control Number: 2015905521
Natural Forces Studio, Mountain Brook, AL

Cover Design - Vicki Schench-atha
Shower Photographs for Indiegogo Campaign- Patrick Carden & Jeremy Lopex

GRATITUDE

"The biggest adventure you can take is to live the
life of your dreams." — OPRAH WINFREY

I dedicate this book to all of you who have gone out in the world against the odds to live your dreams. Thank you for helping me to do my work. But most of all, I hope this helps you to continue doing your work.

Who are you not to shine? You have a gift that is unique to you! Tap into your spirit and shine that purpose!

Thank you to my contributors from the Indiegogo campaign:

Alexander Solomita
@beardedmetsbro
Barry Sayewitz
www.twopansandapot.com
Cindy Heiman
www.rentadaughter.com
Jasper Elliot Wolf
www.consciousbodyyoga.com
Becca Impello
www.sosyoga.com

Marissa Solomita
bestdaughterever!
Ann Lamendola
www.AnnLamendola.com
Virginia Bunting
www.virginiabunting.com
Gail Grossman
www.gailgrossmanyoga.com
Tina Conroy
www.blogtalkradio.com/getintuitwithtinaconroy

Virginia Heiman

Marsha Heiman

Kathy & David Heiman

Mickey Rubenstein

Meredith Pearson

Deborah Rashti

Shannon Andrews

Alyssa Epstein

Rob Bellon

Denie Damico

Brandon Maldonado

Diane Gardsbane

CS Lewis

Jennifer Blostein

Annie Clark

Michael Manley

Randy Sofer

Lauren Mitchell

Alan Heiman

Ingrid Propst

Katie Rogers

Abbey Wallace

Nicholas Nilson

Barbara & Dean DiMaggio

Jennifer Kiselyak Ellwood

Samantha Houston

Megan Lamberti

Jennifer Ellwood

Kewal Nam

Barbara Segal

Jennifer & Clay Dunbar

Lisa Crymes

Tara Fletcher

Barbara Fletcher

Courtney Mitchell

Sherri Romanoff

Leslie Zena Cohen

Contents

Introduction

I remember when I first realized I was tapping in the shower. It wasn't an effort. It wasn't scheduled. I was just following the energy that was needed.

The present issue I was having was overwhelm. I didn't really think this was an issue, just part of my very creative mind. I would wake up, meditate, move through my yoga practice, and then get into the shower.

As I was soaping up, all the many thoughts of my day would come forward. These were all exciting thoughts. As an artist, I have many creative ideas entering my brain, especially after I meditate. But then I would find I was totally overwhelmed with having so much to do because of getting excited with creating. My little brain would get confused with what I was to do first ... second ... third. My list would jumble up because each project was exhilarating and I couldn't wait to jump in.

So, one morning, I decided right then and there, water running, soap covering me, I would just start tapping. I wanted to get back to that peaceful state while I had all this creative energy flowing.

I heard the words ... *overwhelm. Just tap on overwhelm. Otherwise you're not going to get anything done this morning.*

And the rounds of tapping began.

What I noticed was the way in which my energy grounded me. I noticed my list wasn't jumping around anymore.

I remember another morning tapping on *fear*. Again I was in the shower with all my thoughts and allowed the tapping to begin.

Was I really good enough to live my purpose? *tap tap*

Could I let go of my day job and go full-time as a Spiritual Healer? *tap tap tap*

Needless to say, the rounds of tapping went on and on until all the hot water was gone and the water was ice cold. It was time for me to step out.

Tapping, or the Emotional Freedom Technique (EFT), is a simple energy-psychology modality that is at the forefront of alternative healing. It can be used with all kinds of issues as it has profound effects on your emotional and physical health. It is easy to learn and can be used anywhere effectively; it doesn't just have to be in the shower.

EFT works on the amygdala of the brain, the fear center, and immediately lowers the cortisol hormone . . . the stress hormone! By tapping on a series of points on the body as you bring up the emotions, it brings you back to a state of peace and calm. It has been proven to change your responses to old issues.

As I like to say, it takes you from a state of panic into peace in minutes!

According to its teachings, it is one of the few modalities that recognizes that beneath physical problems lies an energy imprint and/or an emotion that is unresolved.

This technique work to remove these imprints and emotional issues and frees us to get out of our own way so we can move forward in life.

Our bodies are made up of many energy meridians that run in and out at various points. This schema supports the flow of prana, our life force. In order to maintain a healthy body, we need to consistently keep a free flow of energy.

On a daily basis, we are confronted with numerous occasions that can throw us off balance and create disturbances within our energy system that block this natural flow of prana.

The basic yet most important premise of this tapping modality comes from Gary Craig, the founder of EFT. He states, "All negative thoughts and emotions come from a disruption in the body's energy system."

This premise means that when you have a negative thought, emotion, or limiting belief, your meridian system is being affected by a physical or emotional issue creating stress and trauma in the body.

There are many layers of stress and trauma. The brain can't tell past from present, big from small — it just reacts! And then we find ourselves bringing up those old energy patterns. We become overwhelmed, stressed out, and paralyzed with fear.

Oh my.

I had originally learned to tap because I was resistant to changing my life. My dad had been injured, my kids were growing up, and I knew I needed to make some changes but found I was fighting any new ideas that I came up with. I also knew that 10 years from then I didn't want to be in the same place.

I had taken courses on EFT, first online with Gary Craig and then in person with Ted Robinson in New York. I attended many of Ted's Borrowing Benefit Groups and training classes. And, most recently, I had taken online courses with Nick and Jessica Ortner of the Tapping Solution.

I had worked with several clients and seen dramatic results with them. I had even noticed the underlying effects it was having on me as I tapped on their issues.

One of the first results I noticed concerned an issue I was having with another woman in my professional circle. Whenever I was around her, I would feel less than who I was. I would shrink and keep my ideas to myself. I finally gave it a name ... *the "D" energy*. If I knew she was going to be at the same meeting or event, I would tap before leaving my house. I would even tap right before going into the program, right at the door! Eventually, the charge of this person was gone. It no longer bothered me. And, even years later, when this feeling comes up with other people I recall the name I gave the energy, do a few rounds of tapping, and ... voila ... it's gone!

But, honestly, I admit the technique looks a little silly. Can you imagine going into a party, all dressed up and standing at the door tapping on points all around yourself? A little ridiculous looking! Even though it was having a great calming effect, I thought it was kind of odd. And I think this is what kept me from exploring the modality even deeper. Until one day, when it all came flooding forward for me when I was in the shower.

I was asking for guidance, praying for help. I knew I had the tools to work it through. I mean, for God's sake, it's what I teach! And that is when I heard the voice within guiding me to tap ... just tap ... just tap.

Why "Confessions of a Shower Tapper"?

A shower tapper is someone who, on a daily basis, uses the Emotional Freedom Technique (tapping) in the shower.

Sometimes it takes stopping and getting really clean with our lives. Washing away the dirt that covers us. Scrubbing away the old layers.

We've got to get out the loofas and many times the pumice stones and really go at it, because it is about removing all those layers of grime that have built up through the years, all those layers that separate us from digging deep into ourselves. It's about finding those truths (which we all have), so that we can bring them out and allow the top layer of our skins to shine.

Water is often referred to in many cultures as the "purifying element" in ceremonies for its cleansing and healing properties.

Tapping in the shower gives us that added benefit and extra layer of vibration. It washes away the fears, the tears, the negative energies, the entities, the thought forms that keep us from living our dreams.

As these negative elements wash away and flow down the shower drain, we bring to the surface a layer of clarity. A clarity that gives us our focus and confidence to keep trying day after day.

I also noticed that the water was washing away all my stress-producing excess energy. And, no one could hear me or see me … I could just tap.

Honestly, you don't have to do this in the shower, but it is a refreshing space to work in, and this is my story.

In the "old school," confessions were often wiped away by an act of reconciliation, such as reciting many prayers in a repetition to release the energy. This can be seen as an exchange of energy or, as I see it, a movement of energy.

Confessions clear the air.

Confessions release attachments to whatever the issue may be.

Confessions mean having to admit your truths by getting really honest with yourself.

Living these truths allows us to commit to living in the present energy, when all is flowing and all is at one with the universe. This is when we can get to the very core of who we are.

Many times we find ourselves very far from our core. We're covered up with so many excuses that we don't even know what exists beneath the surface.

When we can dig into those truths, we can bring forward the things that we are passionate about and uncover the purpose of our life.

Doing our work honestly allows us to admit our truths as we open up to who we truly are. Good, bad, or indifferent, without judgment. Once we begin to live our work honestly, we can live with integrity, which drives our spirit to continually open up.

Think about it. What are your own confessions when it comes to living a life you really want, not someone else's idea of what your life needs to be?

Are you following your passions and desires? Or are you just taking on the family business? Would you choose another profession if fear of being successful wasn't in the way?

Can you confess to wanting more fulfillment in your life? Can you confess to being afraid of your own gifts? Can you confess to stopping yourself from becoming visible with who you are?

In the still of the night, when "those" thoughts pop up, when it's only you listening, what would your confession be?

These are the thoughts that can lead us to living our passions and making a successful living doing it.

As we confess and open up to our authentic selves, we can let go of the illusions that keep us stuck in an old pattern of living.

The chapters ahead will not only offer insight into my thoughts and struggles on living my purpose but also share some universal themes that are common to all of us as we step up to the edge of living a purpose-driven life.

My vision in writing this book was for you to be able to feel supported in removing the many limiting beliefs we all hold in choosing our purpose in living. I want to offer you an energetic way to work them out of your body, mind, and spirit so that your path can become clean, clear, and open.

It's common to one day be on target and the next to feel out of sorts. By applying these techniques in the shower, it reminds us that each day is a new day. It helps us to check in with where we are and acknowledge our emotions. Tapping can become a personal habit, just like the shower.

No emotion is ever final. This book can help you to free the emotions, remove the obstacles by tapping them out and face each day with a clean perspective.

At the end of each chapter are scripts that you, too, can tap on to remove these universal issues out of your tissues as you move forward to living your purpose. Feel free to tap along and even add to the dialogue. It's your life. Find that freedom for yourself!

If you are not familiar with EFT at all, jump to the end of the book and read through the technique on how to tap to get you going.

CONFESSION #1

I've Lost My Spirit

We come into this life with our soul.

We go out of this life with our soul.

Over and over.

Each of us has a *soul vibration* that connects to our spirit.

One of the beautiful things about our souls is that this vibration is at a high level that is unique to each of us. When we slow down, we can begin to tune into this soul vibration to find the resonance that unites us with our divine purpose; the purpose that we are brought into this lifetime to accomplish.

As we continuously tune into the spirit and live this vibration, any and everything can be accomplished. I believe this to be a Universal Law.

I know this. I practice this. I teach this.

Yet ... here is my first confession.

There are many times that I lose this vibration. I forget all about my spirit, and my mind gets the best of me. I become stuck with thoughts that block this vibration from allowing me to fully live my purpose in life.

And, so I find myself in the shower ... tapping.

At the karate-chop point: *Even though I forget I have a strong spirit, I completely love and accept myself.*

Even though I allow limiting thoughts to overtake my spirit, I completely love and accept myself.

Even though I forget the power of my spirit, I completely love and accept myself.

And then the rounds of tapping begin.

At the eyebrow: *These thoughts.*

Sides of the eyes: *These thoughts.*

Underneath the eye: *These thoughts that get in the way of living my purpose.*

Underneath the nose: *These thoughts that stop me from living my purpose.*

On the chin: *These thoughts that doubt this universal truth.*

Collarbone: *These thoughts that limit me from helping myself as I have been taught to help others.*

Underneath the armpit: *These thoughts that aren't mine.*

Top of the head: *These thoughts that arise from listening to others.*

At the eyebrow: *These thoughts that come from the mass consciousness telling me to be a certain way.*

Sides of the eyes: *These thoughts that drain my energy.*

Underneath the eyes: *These thoughts that get in the way of my spirit.*

Underneath the nose: *I'll never do it.*

On the chin: *I can't even hear my own purpose.*

Collarbone: *But I know it's in there, somewhere.*

Underneath the armpit: *Where is my spirit today?*

Top of the head: *It's within me ... it's within me ... it's within me.*

Back to the karate chop point: *I love and accept myself.*

I release my hands and I take a deep breath. I feel the water rushing down my back.

As I tap and bring up my story, my issues wash down the shower drain. I allow the purifying energy of the water to wash over me and cleanse it all out. And then I step out ... out of the shower and into my life ... whole and ready for my day.

CONFESSION #2

I'm Scared To Death

Not too long ago, trusting my purpose in life, I began to think about letting go of my "day job." Now this day job was creative and artistic but it wasn't living what I would call my true calling, my mission in life. I had spent close to two decades as a single mother working at a job to pay my bills while I was raising my children. The time had come for me to make a change in my life. Believing in this universal law of connecting with my divine purpose, I took the leap of faith.

I finally let go of my day job.

I took some money from my savings account and began my healing arts practice, full time.

I'm excited! I'm thrilled to be doing this work, helping others, serving a spiritual calling.

But then there are days when nothing is going as I had planned. The phone isn't ringing. My studio has been quiet all week. I begin to feel the panic and fear rise up. I'm scared the phone will never ring again.

I recognize that it's not really about my work. I've studied in the Healing Arts for many years; I've had my own counseling. I am certified in the energy modalities that I teach. I do indeed know my craft.

The problem lies on the subconscious level, which is ultimately where the work needs to be done!

Somewhere in my past as a little girl, I was told by one teacher or another to pay attention to the blackboard, to quit asking questions, to quit dreaming, to sit a certain way, and to be like everyone else.

EFT works because the conscious mind doesn't have to determine where the issue is coming from, when or why it happened in order to resolve the emotions. We only have to acknowledge the emotion or physical pain and begin tapping.

Tapping on specific energy points of the body is what breaks it all up and gets the energy and emotions flowing again in the way you want it to flow.

The simplicity in EFT is that we really don't need to diagnose the problem. We simply acknowledge what emotion we are feeling in the moment and address it by tapping on the given energy meridians one by one as we allow the flow of energy to return.

EFT teaches us that as we acknowledge our emotions, we tell the subconscious mind that although we have this emotion we (the conscious mind) accept it. This offers relief to the subconscious mind that it is being validated by the more-present self. And this is where it all starts.

Can you imagine how scary it must be for me to find myself feeling so afraid about the very thing that I am teaching others to do … to tune into their purpose and find their mission in life to live it … full time?

And I wind up in the shower once again.

At the karate-chop point: *Even though I know I have this true calling, I am scared, but I love and accept myself.*

Even though I have so much fear, I love and accept myself.

Even though I'm scared shitless to live my purpose, I love and accept myself.

At the eyebrow: *This fear of living my life.*

Side of the eye: *This fear that my purpose isn't good enough.*

Underneath the eye: *That I'm not good enough.*

Under the nose: *This fear that I won't make enough money.*

On the chin: *This fear that stops me from moving forward with my work.*

Collarbone: *This fear I'll never make it.*

Underneath the armpit: *This fear that no one will work with me.*

Top of the head: *This fear of sinking in a hole …*

I keep tapping around and around and around, repeating the same words, feeling a little peace enter in. I know that when I work from a place of peace and calm, I allow the authenticity of my work to come forward, not the ego of my mind. And this, I believe, is where I can best serve and help others.

But this morning, fear has taken over. I'm scared shitless about my own purpose, not to mention helping others with their directions in life.

And so I find myself moving through a few more rounds of tapping. Sometimes there is still some lingering energy that reminds me to tap some more. So what if I am running out of hot water!? I'll just keep tapping.

Karate chop point: *Even though I'm scared to death and have so much fear, I love and accept myself.*

Even though it feels like I'm a fraud and don't know my work, I love and accept myself.

Even though I feel scared to be tapping on what I am teaching, I love myself completely.

At the eyebrow: *Feeling scared to be tapping on what I am teaching.*

Side of the eye: *Feeling like I don't know my purpose if I am tapping on it.*

Underneath the eye: *People will think I am a fraud.*

Underneath the nose: *I'm scared I'm not any good.*

On the chin: *I'm going to look like a fool.*

Collarbone: *I'm supposed to be the expert.*

Underneath the armpit: *But I have my own fears.*

Top of the head: *It's scary to be living my purpose, 'cause I have issues, too.*

Eyebrow point: *We all have issues.*

Side of the eye: *We all continue to grow in our work.*

Underneath the eye: *That's what life is about.*

Underneath the nose: *We teach what we need to learn ourselves.*

On the chin: *That's how we grow. Every day we learn.*

Collarbone: *It's a process.*

Underneath the armpit: *Fear is only false evidence appearing real.*

Top of the head: *I know this. I can do this.*

Back to the karate-chop point: *I love and accept myself.*

I release my hands and I take a deep breath.

I feel the water rushing down my back.

Finally, I can dry off as I step out and begin my day of helping others.

CONFESSION #3

I'm Not Lovable

I'm not lovable, so how can I live my purpose?

I'm not in a relationship.

I confess to not having had sex in months.

I've had a horrible divorce.

Two, to be exact.

I'm just not lovable.

No one wants me. May as well eat those worms.

I may as well stay invisible until I meet someone.

Don't we all need someone to make us worthy?

Isn't that what society tells us?

Wait … what about loving myself?

Isn't that where I need to start!?

Even using the phrase *I love and accept myself* is hard to do. But it feels good to say it, even if I doubt it.

We all have to start somewhere ... right?

And starting by loving ourselves is a great place to begin.

How can we love others if we can't love ourselves?

How can we expect to be in a relationship if we don't have love for ourselves?

How can we go out into the world and live our purpose if we don't have love for ourselves?

And so my morning ritual begins. I get in the shower. I turn the water on.

At the karate-chop point: *Even though I'm having a hard time loving and accepting myself, I love and accept myself.*

Even though I have no one to love me, I love and accept myself.

Even though I'm not in a relationship, I love and accept myself.

At the eyebrow point: *I'll never be loved.*

Side of the eye: *No one will ever love me.*

Underneath the eye: *I'm just not lovable.*

Underneath the nose: *Not lovable.*

On the chin: *No one is ever going to love me.*

Underneath the nose: *Why not?*

Collarbone: *I might as well give up.*

Underneath the armpit: *I don't know how to love.*

Top of the head: *I don't know how to let someone love me.*

At the eyebrow point: *But I want to be loved.*

Side of the eye: *We all need love.*

Underneath the eye: *I'll just love myself.*

Underneath the nose: *But I'm not lovable.*

On the chin: *But I can love me.*

Collarbone: *I can love me.*

Underneath the armpit: *I do love me.*

Top of the head: *I'll start with that.*

At the eyebrow point: *I'll love myself first.*

Side of the eye: *Then others can love me.*

Underneath the eye: *And I can be loved.*

Underneath the nose: *Be love.*

On the chin: *Be love.*

Collarbone: *Be love.*

Underneath the armpit: *Be love and live my purpose.*

Top of the head: *I am love.*

Back to the karate-chop point: *I love and accept myself.*

I release my hands and I take a deep breath. I feel the water rushing down my back.

Love is the greatest vibration. When we can love ourselves we allow others to love us right back! This phrase, *I love and accept myself,* has a twofold effect. We can learn to love ourself and tell the brain at the same time! Then we can allow this vibration to extend out all around us.

CONFESSION #4

I'm Searching on the Outside

L iving one's purpose is not always the easiest path. It can be hard and challenging. It can even be a little frightening out there in the world, especially when everyone else is thinking, *What is she doing? Why doesn't she just get a job?*

So much of our childhood has conditioned us to be like everyone else. Get up ... go to work ... come home ... do it all over again.

How many times have you heard someone saying to you, "Go to school, get an education, be a doctor, a lawyer or some other professional type"?

Or maybe it's, "Carry on the family business whether you want to or not."

And so our dreams get pushed down, our spirit is forgotten about, until one morning we wake up very depressed and unhappy.

So many times, this depression and unhappiness leads to a search outside ourselves. That dissatisfaction with our lives keeps surfacing. We turn to the quick fixes: drugs, alcohol, antidepressants, shopping, eating—all of which only take us further away from our spirit rather than tuning into it.

For me, it's always been about either overeating or overspending.

I can't just have one of anything. Nope. Must have at least two or more ... just in case.

Constantly stuffing down the real feelings.

I'm searching for the next outfit to make me look good just in case I get called to do something. Or I'm buying more food to make myself feel better. Only the quick fixes aren't even helping; they only make me more discontent with myself.

If only we would just stop and pull all that energy in. Slow down. But it is so much easier to keep searching outside of ourselves. The quick fixes give us that instant feeling of being OK.

Here comes that shower again, before I can even allow myself to go shopping.

At the karate-chop point: *Even though I know I am searching on the surface level for help, I love and accept myself completely.*

Even though I keep looking everywhere else except within, I love and accept myself completely.

Even though I'm overeating and overspending, not feeling better, I love and accept myself completely.

At the eyebrow: *All this searching on the outside is getting to me.*

Side of the eyes: *I just keep shopping and shopping.*

Underneath the eye: *I'm so afraid to stop it.*

Underneath the nose: *I shop for clothes ... for food ... for more books than I can read.*

On the chin: *I'm afraid to look within.*

Collarbone: *I'm afraid to sit with myself.*

Underneath the armpit: *I'm afraid to slow down.*

Top of the head: *This fear that keeps me from living my purpose may surface instead.*

At the eyebrow: *It's fear that keeps me searching.*

Side of the eyes: *I keep looking out there for answers.*

Underneath the eyes: *I keep looking out there for acknowledgment.*

Underneath the nose: *I just want someone to tell me I look nice.*

On the chin: *I want some acknowledgment.*

Collarbone: *I really must listen to my deeper desire, not to others.*

Underneath the armpit: *That's where the power is.*

Top of the head: *It's not out there. It's within me. It's within me.*

Back to the karate-chop point: *I love and accept myself.*

I release my hands and I take a deep breath. I feel the water rushing down my back.

I notice I've washed away the discontent. The hot water gets through that surface layer of dirt. I can hear my own voice coming from within. It's time to step out and begin my day of living my purpose from the inside out.

CONFESSION #5

I'm Listening to Others

I have discovered that, as I stand on my edge and put my work out into the universe, there are times when I feel uneasy or nervous.

Being raised in the Bible Belt, I had an overall feeling of the fear of God. Either you believed in the "new" testament or you would be sentenced to ... well ... hell.

Growing up in a southern Jewish community, the messages were even more confusing. Stay in your community. Be with your own chosen people. Don't wander out.

It led me to keep quiet about my personal beliefs for fear of being different and going to well ... somewhere that I didn't belong... like a hell.

So... you can imagine the looks I got when I returned to the South after 35 years of education in the North and spoke about being an Interfaith Minister of Spiritual Counseling with a southern Jewish background practicing yoga and teaching energy work.

What!

Yep ... that's me. It all comes down to a very inclusive teaching of *all is one*. We are all coming from the same oneness.

Teaching spiritual development is not the norm, and I recognize that I am opening myself up to lots of comments from others. Even a basic, "Why are you doing that, especially living in the Bible Belt?" can trigger a long list of emotional reactions.

People say to me, "Shhh! Better not say what you are doing too loud. It's just not accepted down here." Or they say to me, "You can't be spiritual. You need a religion in the South." Or even, "Isn't that the devil's work that you are teaching?"

Without my even knowing it, these kind of comments can trigger a response within me, and I notice a shift in my energy. All of a sudden I am scattered in my thoughts and I find myself procrastinating on moving forward with my projects. I find myself making all kinds of excuses and pulling back from what I really want — until, all of a sudden, I find myself confessing in the shower once again.

At the karate-chop point: *Even though I know I am listening to other people's opinions, I love and accept myself completely.*

Even though I know I am not listening to my spirit, I love and accept myself completely.

Even though I know I am letting other people's opinions matter more than mine, I love and accept myself completely.

At the eyebrow: *Everyone's opinion is better than mine.*

Side of the eye: *Everyone knows better than me.*

Underneath the eye: *No they don't … yes they do … no they don't … yes they do.*

Underneath the nose: *It's just easier to ask others what to do.*

On the chin: *Why should I listen to myself? I haven't been in the South for over 35 years.*

On the collarbone: *But it's my life, not theirs.*

Underneath the armpit: *I know my spirit.*

Top of the head: *But maybe they do know.*

Eyebrow point: *I know my spirit better than anyone ... I can listen to myself.*

Side of the eye: *I can listen.*

Underneath the eye: *I know my thoughts.*

Underneath the nose: *I do hear them.*

On the chin: *It's my spirit guiding me.*

Collarbone: *It's my spirit talking to me when everything is quiet.*

Underneath the armpit: *That's where I get my strength.*

Top of the head: *From me ... it comes from me ... it comes from within me.*

Back to the karate-chop point: *I love and accept myself.*

I release my hands and I take a deep breath. I feel the water rushing down my back.

I step out, and my day of listening to me begins.

CONFESSION #6

I'm Not Trusting My Work

Today is a bathtub day!

It was a morning of tears and swearing. The kind of day where the self just isn't standing up. Only the fears, the worries, the *I'm not authentic … I can't do it … What good is my work?* kind of day.

I am doubting my work. All I can hear in my head is, *If I can't do this work and manifest my results, how can I help anyone else? If I am doubting my own intuition, how can I teach anyone else to trust their intuition? What good am I, anyway?*

I'm not trusting any of my decisions right now.

And I call myself an Intuitive!

But am I really?

Where does all that info come from?

I get the hits.

I can see them in my third eye.

So why don't I trust it?

Not everyone can do this.

So why do I fear it?

Why do I doubt it?

I never doubt Reiki energy.

I can't see it but I know it's there.

It's running the groove. The same questions over and over. I've heard them already. I've answered them already. Why do I keep listening to this voice of my ego all the time?

Where is my intuition?

This is my work. It's what I do best.

I teach it to others.

So much doubt.

Why does the ego keep wanting to take over?

It seems the tears fill my bath. They just keep falling and falling, which is actually the best time to tap. The emotions are already on the edge of the surface, making it easier to pull them up and out of the body. On that subjective understanding of distress scale (SUD) from 1 to 10, I am definitely at a 10. Knowing this is the highest level of distress, I find that karate-chop point through my tears.

At the karate-chop point: *Even though I'm not trusting my work, I love and accept myself completely.*

Even though I am questioning my own intuition, I love and accept myself completely.

Even though I know I am letting my ego get in my way, I love and accept myself completely.

At the eyebrow point: *I don't trust my intuition.*

Side of the eye: *My ego is getting in the way.*

Underneath the eye: *How can I teach others to trust their intuition if I am not trusting mine?*

Underneath the nose: *I have vision.*

On the chin: *But I'm not trusting it.*

On the collarbone: *I should just give up.*

Underneath the armpit: *Why won't my ego stop this nonsense?*

Top of the head: *My mind is so full of chatter. How can I teach others when I am still learning to trust myself?*

At the eyebrow point: *I am not trusting my program.*

Side of the eyes: *I'm not trusting my inner guidance.*

Underneath the eye: *I'm not trusting my gifts and abilities.*

Underneath the nose: *I am psychic.*

On the chin: *I know things.*

Collarbone: *But I'm not trusting it.*

Underneath the armpit: *Maybe it's not even there.*

Top of the head: *But I do have inner guidance.*

At the eyebrow point: *Why do I doubt it?*

Side of the eyes: *But I keep listening to my ego.*

Underneath the eye: *It keeps me spinning.*

Underneath the nose: *I need to trust my intuition.*

On the chin: *My intuition is what guides me to make my decisions.*

On the collarbone: *Trust that intuition.*

Underneath the armpit: *I can trust it.*

Top of the head: *I have a knowing.*

Eyebrow point: *It is within.*

Side of the eyes: *Move out of the way, ego.*

Underneath the eyes: *Take a break, ego.*

Underneath the nose: *Trust … trust … trust.*

On the chin: *My intuition is right on.*

Collarbone: *I know it is.*

Underneath the armpit: *I teach others how to trust their intuition.*

Top of the head: *I have the knowing and inner guidance.*

I take a deep breath and notice the full tub of water. I pull the drain plug, but I'm not ready to get out.

Back to the karate-chop point: *Even though I've moved a little energy and I am doubting my work, I love and accept myself completely.*

Even though I know I've moved a little energy and I am still not trusting my own abilities, I love and accept myself completely.

Even though I know I am letting my ego get in my way, I love and accept myself completely.

At the eyebrow point: *I'm not trusting my own work.*

Side of the eye: *I doubt my own intuition.*

Underneath the eye: *I'll never be able to teach others to use their intuition if I am doubting mine.*

Underneath the nose: *But I know I am clairvoyant. I have psychic abilities.*

On the chin: *I know I can see, but why do I doubt it?*

On the collarbone: *I should just give up ... no trust ... no faith.*

Underneath the armpit: *Who am I trusting?*

Top of the head: *How can I teach others when I am still doubting myself?*

Eyebrow point: *I don't trust my inner voice.*

Side of the eye: *I need to trust that inner voice.*

Underneath the eye: *Let go of the ego.*

Underneath the nose: *I know things!*

On the chin: *I don't have to doubt it.*

Collarbone: *I have great intuition.*

Underneath the armpit: *Maybe it's not even there? If I doubt, so will my students.*

Top of the head: *I won't even have any students ... oh gosh ... I need more rounds of tapping!*

At the eyebrow point: *Not trusting ... This doubt ... Isn't this how we all learn?*

Side of the eye: *I am intuitive.*

Underneath the eye: *We teach what we need to learn ourselves.*

Underneath the nose: *This is my path.*

On the chin: *My inner guidance is telling me now.*

On the collarbone: *I shouldn't give up ... trust.*

Underneath the armpit: *Everyone goes through doubt when they are starting out.*

Top of the head: *This is normal. My spirit is just challenging me.*

Eyebrow point: *It is strong, I can trust.*

Side of the eye: *I know I can.*

Underneath the eye: *It is alive within.*

Underneath the nose: *I am intuitive.*

On the chin: *I can read energy.*

Collarbone: *I don't need this doubt. I can trust my knowing.*

Underneath the armpit: *My intuition is strong ... I can trust it.*

Top of the head: *I can live my purpose ... I can see ... I can have faith ... I am strong.*

Back to the karate-chop point: *I love and accept myself.*

I release my hands and I take a deep breath.

The tub is empty, my self-doubt has drained out with the water, and my trust within has returned. I can get out now and dry off.

As I step out of the shower I recall a quote I printed off Facebook that's taped on my computer. It says: "She was unstoppable, not because she didn't have failures or doubts, but because she continued on despite them."

I'm Letting the Wounded Child Take Over

Today is a different day. *Isn't every day?* Yet, as I get into my morning shower, I reflect on yesterday's bath ... *who was that talking?*

It must have been that wounded child within me. It's a part of me that pops up when I am being challenged in my work and it surfaces when I am trying something new. Something is triggered deep within that sends my mind into a tailspin.

Unresolved emotional issues can dominate us and rule our lives. Very often we store these beliefs deep in our subconscious mind. As we grow up, whenever an experience gets near to feeling like something from our past, our wounded child arises and begins to take over.

We become stuck, and our energy system becomes disturbed.

Most often, we are not even aware that this is what is happening to us.

We just think it is our true self when, actually, it's quite the opposite. It's an old self that arises, one that has around the emotional intelligence of a toddler.

Somewhere in my past I was told to stick to the rules, to color within the lines, or that I wasn't good enough to be on the cheerleading squad. Actually, it doesn't really matter what it was. All I know is that I am feeling a force rising up that is taking over and feels so out of place.

And I am listening to it.

Instead of taking charge, I am allowing it to take charge of me. Gosh, that wounded child is full of fear, and that fear has been held in the body for ages. Was that energy ever resolved?

I know if I just tap, the scenarios will start to come up and I can tap on the energy points to release the issues that trap and bind me from moving forward. But I don't want to. I have resistance here.

Once I can clear the meridians, I know energy will flow again.

I know with EFT, without even having to understand why, I can tap this out of the body to get the energy flowing again and back to trusting my work as valuable and worth its price, without any judgment. Hmmmm ... judgment ... that's another facet of the wounded child ... something else to tap on, too.

I know this, yet it is so hard for me to tap this morning.

I've also seen the amazing and healing way that EFT has busted through so many things. I know it's just the limiting beliefs of the wounded child that are getting in my way to success and financial freedom. Yet I still can't make myself tap this morning.

What is wrong with me? Tapping will help rid all those limited blocks right out of the body and raise my wealth consciousness immediately.

It's just that this wounded child keeps showing up. *Color in the lines ... don't try anything new ... not good enough to be picked ... and so on and so on.*

I keep noticing that I am talking myself out of making new decisions with my life.

Like yesterday, so much chitchat going on in my head all the time.

It's just so easy to let that part of my ego take over.

But … if I could just start tapping on the energy meridians of the body, I could get those electrical impulses connecting and break up these disturbances so that the energy could be moving in an abundant flow.

I could release the trapped emotions that have been stored in my body for ages. I'm aware I have these, but many times I have no idea that I am working with these old, limiting beliefs.

It's almost like I am two different people.

All I recognize is that I'm not creating the results I want.

I just need to find that karate-chop point and just start. Yes, just start.

At the karate-chop point: *Even though this wounded child is getting in my way, I love and accept myself completely.*

Even though I know I am not me right now, I love and accept myself completely.

Even though I know the wounded child is getting in my way, I love and accept myself completely.

At the eyebrow point: *It's that wounded child.*

Side of the eye: *That wounded child is getting in my way.*

Underneath the eye: *What's wrong with me?*

Underneath the nose: *That wounded child is getting in my way.*

On the chin: *I feel like I'm in second grade again.*

Collarbone: *I won't listen to her. I'll just keep tapping.*

Underneath the armpit: *It's just the voice of a little girl, not me.*

Top of the head: *The real me is strong. I can let this other voice inside go. I choose to let it go.*

Eyebrow point: *I can be picked for the team. I can be a cheerleader, too.*

Side of the eye: *No, I won't. I'll never make the squad.*

Underneath the eye: *It's just a very young voice.*

Underneath the nose: *But I keep hearing her over and over.*

On the chin: *Pick me, pick me. I'll do whatever you want.*

Collarbone: *I'll work harder than anyone and give more than everyone.*

Underneath the armpit: *I was picked for the team ... once.*

Top of the head: *That was a very long time ago.*

At the eyebrow point: *That wounded child is from a very long time ago.*

Side of the eye: *I acknowledge her and let her go.*

Underneath the eye: *I send her love.*

Underneath the nose: *Lots of love.*

On the chin: *Lots of love.*

Collarbone: *I am strong. I am strong and loved.*

Underneath the armpit: *My voice is strong. I am my own cheerleader.*

Top of the head: *I can let this other voice inside go … I choose me.*

Eyebrow point: *I choose to live my purpose.*

Side of the eye: *I choose to be present now.*

Underneath the eye: *I am good at what I do.*

Underneath the nose: *I can be a leader.*

On the chin: *I can let the wounds go.*

Collarbone: *I choose others to be on my team.*

Underneath the armpit: *I have a strong team to work with.*

Top of the head: *I am a strong woman.*

Back to the karate-chop point: *I love and accept myself.*

I release my hands and I take a deep breath. I feel the water rushing down my back.

I know I am good at what I do. I know I never wanted to be cheering for football players, anyway. I can cheer for me. I can pick me in the story of my life.

CONFESSION #8

I Have Self-Limiting Beliefs

L ack of confidence is getting the best of me today. I know it's a process. From one year to the next, we ride the wave, adjusting to the endless changes in our lives, always trying to stay grounded, be positive, and feel good … but it's a struggle at times.

My self-limiting beliefs are so quick to surface. They knock me off my feet.

How many years do I have to keep running from that artist within me?

First it was, *I don't have the struggling-artist abilities, so I'll never make it as a dancer in the arts*. And then it was, *The world doesn't need another jewelry designer, so I'll be a healer*. And now it's, *I'll never make money as a healer*. But as I look at the whole picture, I've been running from the arts forever because of my own self-limiting beliefs. I've been spinning in the same circle.

I work in the Healing Arts, helping people to heal their spirit, no matter what medium I choose. I have finally come to realize that no matter how I look or don't look at it, I am an artist. My work is layered with many levels of creative modalities.

You walk into my studio and my artwork is on the walls. My healing jewelry is in my case. My beautiful Reiki table is open. Why do I keep avoiding my gifts? Why am I limiting myself all the time by thinking I can't make money with these passionate pursuits of mine? Natural healing requires that artistic side of the brain.

Why do I keep hearing, *You'll never make money as a healer?* Aren't these the same thoughts that I had 35 years ago when I first moved to New York and wanted to be a dancer? Aren't these the same self-limiting beliefs that said to me then, *You can't survive as a dancer ... change your work ... you can't survive as a jewelry designer ... change your work ... you can't survive as a healer ... change your work.* But now there isn't anything to change to!

But I just keep hearing, *It's going to be a huge challenge and will take lots of effort.*

Life is a struggle.

You've got to work really hard.

You can't be spiritual and make money, too.

Where did all those thoughts come from?

These self-limiting beliefs are the stories that we keep telling ourselves. These thoughts impact the choices we make and how we behave in any given situation.

These negative thoughts make us feel powerless to make new choices because our sense of reality is limited by these old beliefs.

They can be extremely powerful because they disconnect the relationship between the neural pathways in our brain. And they are low-vibrational energy imprints. They aren't going to help us move beyond the old thinking. They are imprints of fear, doubt, stress, and anxiety, all of which keep us from moving forward, no matter how much we want to.

They come from our family, friends, co-workers, religious institutions, and the mass consciousness.

The only purpose they serve is to block the meridians in our energy system, stopping the natural flow of abundant energy. So we become stuck in old patterns without even realizing it.

Anytime an experience brings us even close to feeling like we're about to be challenged in our work, these self-limiting beliefs pop up and create a powerful, fear-based reality.

These self-limiting beliefs are also tied to that wounded child of yesterday.

Start the shower! Get the soap! This woman needs to feel the water on her face.

At the karate-chop point: *Even though I keep hearing all these self-limiting beliefs, I love and accept myself completely.*

Even though I keep listening to all these self-limiting beliefs, I love and accept myself completely.

Even though I keep listening to all these self-limiting beliefs, I love and accept myself completely.

At the eyebrow point: *All these self-limiting beliefs.*

Side of the eye: *All these self-limiting beliefs just get in my way.*

Underneath the eye: *These self-limiting beliefs aren't real, so why do I listen to them?*

Underneath the nose: *They are just old self-limiting beliefs. I'll never make it as an artist. Never make it as an artist … never.*

On the chin: *Never make money being an artist.*

Collarbone: *Beliefs that don't serve my purpose.*

Underneath the armpit: *They are just beliefs that come from my family or friends or co-workers. I can hear them now. Who do you think you are?*

Top of the head: *I choose to let them go.*

At the eyebrow point: *All these self-limiting beliefs.*

Side of the eye: *But life is so hard, and it takes money to live.*

Underneath the eye: *But it doesn't have to be so hard.*

Underneath the nose: *But it is.*

On the chin: *No, I can go with the flow of life.*

Collarbone: *Life can be easy and effortless doing what I love. It's my passion.*

Underneath the armpit: *I can make money living my purpose … being spiritual … helping others.*

Top of the head: *These self-limiting beliefs no longer serve me. I choose to let them go. I can live my passion and be as artistic as I choose. And I choose to let them go.*

Back to the karate-chop point: *I love and accept myself.*

I release my hands and I take a deep breath. I feel the water rushing down my back.

I turn the water off and, as I get out of the shower, I notice the art hanging on the wall. It's my creation, and I love it.

CONFESSION #9

I Keep Comparing Myself to Others

Why is it every time I go on Facebook, I find myself sinking into a hole? Everyone looks so perfect and like they are doing such great work.

Why can't I be like the Goddess Entrepreneur or the Chakra Warrior or the Ninja?

I can't ever come up with anything so clever!

Does the world even need another healer?

What do I have to offer that someone else isn't already doing?

There are already so many great people out there teaching Reiki, offering treatments, reading Angel cards, offering intuitive healings, working with crystals and essential oils. I'm no different.

Maybe I need to learn another modality. Craniosacral seems to be popular now. That's it! Another modality to learn and then offer. That's what I'll do, and then I can add another category onto my website and have even more to offer and more choices for people.

But, wait a minute.

I just started learning Pranic Healing last year. Why don't I go deeper with that?

But that other healer seems to always have a booked schedule offering craniosacral treatments. I know I need to be like her.

Whoa! Time to wash that idea right down the drain. I've already got so many great skills to share ... no need to compare.

Let's turn that water on.

At the karate-chop point: *Even though I've been comparing myself to other people, I love and accept myself.*

Even though I've been so hard on myself, I love and accept myself.

Even though I've been comparing myself to other people, I love and accept myself.

At the eyebrow point: *Does the world really need another healer?*

Side of the eye: *Is another Reiki Master really needed?*

Underneath the eye: *There are already so many healers out there.*

Underneath the nose: *What's so unique about me?*

On the chin: *Why do I always have to compare myself to others?*

Collarbone: *It leaves me frustrated and discouraged.*

Underneath the armpit: *But the other healers seem to always be booked ... their groups are always filled.*

Top of the head: *Yeah, but look at my own studio ... look at the sacred space I create.*

At the eyebrow point: *I love my studio. It is different than others' ... all my artwork is hanging.*

Side of the eye: *But does the world need another artist? I remember saying that and changing my work. I can't keep switching my profession.*

Underneath the eye: *Stop comparing myself to others. It just makes me frustrated.*

Underneath the nose: *Stop comparing. I have my own unique gifts and my own vibration. People who need me will resonate to me.*

On the chin: *My work may not be for everyone, but there are plenty who it will serve.*

Collarbone: *I no longer need to make any comparisons. I have my own unique gifts to share. No need to compare.*

Underneath the armpit: *I can go deeper and get really clear and powerful about what I offer.*

Top of the head: *I do have my own "blue ocean." I don't need to compare.*

Back to the karate-chop point: *I love and accept myself.*

I release my hands and I take a deep breath. I feel the water rushing down my back.

The water drains away with all the dirty residue that goes with comparing myself to others. It is so not needed. I trust my own unique abilities. It's like the soaps I buy. There are so many out there, yet I always seem to find the one that is just perfect for me. What if the world only made one type of soap?

My studio and my work reflects my "blue ocean," as Professors Kim and Mauborgne talk about in their book, *"Blue Ocean Strategy".* There really isn't anyone else like me out there.

I think I have a new mantra: *I have my own unique gifts to share … no need to compare.* It's tweetable.

CONFESSION #10

I Can't Charge that Much Money

Why did I charge so much for my program?

It's too much.

How can I be spiritual and charge that much to help someone?

But there is a lot of value in what I am offering.

But am I worth it?

Can people really see that? There is a lot to my packages. They're complete.

Why did I have to put so much info into my programs?

I'm not going to attract anyone.

But it's never really about the money.

I always find it if I really want it.

I'll lower the price. That will work. I'll just give it away for half.

Isn't that the best option? Lower the price, sell it for less!

Oh hell. While I'm at it, why don't I just give it away this first year? For free! Then I don't have to "sell" anyone! That will make it so easy ... and so off-balance!

Where the heck is my self-worth? I mean, come on, woman. You know this. There always has to be an energetic exchange!

I know this all the way to the very bottom of my soul, yet the issues come up. I jump in the shower quick before any of this attaches to me. I don't even wait for the water to flow as I begin to tap.

At the karate-chop point: *Even though I waver in my self-worth, I love and accept myself completely.*

Even though I am questioning the money, I love and accept myself completely.

Even though I have this fear of charging money, I love and accept myself completely.

At the eyebrow point: *No self worth.*

Side of the eye: *I can't give away my work.*

Underneath the eye: *Oh, just this first time.*

Underneath the nose: *Just give it away for free.*

On the chin: *No, I can't do that.*

Collarbone: *Just charge less.*

Underneath the armpit: *Just charge a little.*

Top of the head: *Charge a lot ... Charge a little ... Charge nothing.*

Eyebrow: *It's not about the money.*

Side of the eye: *Then what's it about?*

Underneath the eye: *It's never about the money.*

Underneath the nose: *I always found the money when I wanted something.*

On the chin: *Money comes from source. Source is the Universe and the Universe is abundant!*

Collarbone: *Find the balance of money and work.*

Underneath the armpit: *Money is an energy.*

Top of the head: *My work is right on and worth the dollars.*

Eyebrow: *My work is good.*

Side of the eye: *It's about how I perceive my own value.*

Underneath the eye: *My value in the marketplace.*

Underneath the nose: *My work serves many.*

On the chin: *I can charge for it.*

Collarbone: *Yes, I am worth it.*

Underneath the armpit: *But it's not about me.*

Top of the head: *It's about my work.*

Eyebrow: *But then I have to call people and sell it to them.*

Side of the eye: *But is it selling or is it helping?*

Underneath the eye: *Selling or helping?*

Underneath the nose: *My work serves many.*

On the chin: *I can make that call. I can charge for it.*

Collarbone: *Yes, I am worth it and my work helps many!*

Underneath the armpit: *I can call and I can serve others.*

Top of the head: *And I can charge real dollars for it!*

Back to the karate-chop point: *I love and accept myself.*

I release my hands and I take a deep breath.

I realize I never even turned on the water. So now, I turn on the tap and let the water flow down my back and cleanse my spirit of all this chatter. I let all this excess energy just wash down the drain. The water not only cleans me but also cleanses away this subtle layer of energy as it reveals a much shinier skin to guide me through my day.

I notice how much more connected I am to spirit at this moment. I have found the worth within my own spirit. The more I believe in my own self-worth, the more others will, too. It's never about the money.

Making money can be spiritual. It's what you choose to do with the money that counts. I realize that the more money I make, the more I can help others. And then they go on to serve and it keeps going!

There's nothing wrong with this.

I also realize that if I continue to give away my work for free it keeps me stuck in this lack vibration and then it's very hard to break away from from giving my work for free.

Sometimes we may not have enough experience so we think, "I won't charge as much" — but this perpetuates the pattern. We have to take that plunge and trust in the work, especially when it is spiritual and serves humanity.

I am worth it ... and you are, too!

CONFESSION #11

I'm Overwhelmed With My Life

I just love my mornings spent in meditation. I love the peace and serenity that come from being still. It really allows me the time to connect with my purpose and know that I am on the right path.

The breathing calms me down.

The yoga postures are good for my physical body.

And now it's time to face my desk … calm and collected.

So many things to do.

What's first?

Let's see … write the copy … schedule the event … shoot the photos … call the clients … email my list … OMG!

Maybe I will just take a break. Time for a coffee break. No matter that it is only five minutes into my day.

I just don't know where to start.

I'll start with coffee and make a list.

So many things to put on that list that I don't even know where to start it.

Where's that coffee?

If only I could just ground myself a little bit.

Maybe I will just take a day off. That would help. I work for myself, anyway. I can do whatever I want!

Wait a minute. I can't really afford to take a day off in the middle of all these preparations. I just had a nice weekend.

I am so overwhelmed with all the details to get done that I can't decide what to do first, second, or third.

Help!

Where is that calm mind? Where is that peace that I was just experiencing?

It's clouded by all the details I need to do.

Isn't this where I started with tapping, anyway?

I did my meditation … yoga … but now it's all the things I'm excited about doing. They keep rushing to the forefront of my mind. I'm excited about all my projects, but I can't decide what I want to do first. I feel like I waste so much time trying to figure it out that half the morning goes by without accomplishing anything.

I think I will take a step back and jump into the shower, clean up, do a round of tapping on overwhelm, and then get dressed for the day.

At the karate-chop point: *Even though I am so overwhelmed, I love and accept myself completely.*

Even though I'm not grounded very well this morning, I love and accept myself completely.

Even though I am so overwhelmed, I love and accept myself completely.

At the eyebrow point: *Feeling very overwhelmed.*

Side of the eye: *Feeling very ungrounded.*

Underneath the eye: *I don't know where to begin.*

Underneath the nose: *I'm so excited about all my projects that I want to do this all at once.*

On the chin: *But then I can't get anything done.*

Collarbone: *This cycle continues, and I get nothing done.*

Underneath the armpit: *Might as well take a break to figure it all out.*

Top of the head: *Wait ... my day just started ... I can't do that.*

At the eyebrow point: *I'm so overwhelmed.*

Side of the eye: *But if I just start with one thing.*

Underneath the eye: *There is power in getting just one thing done.*

Underneath the nose: *And then I can get the next thing done.*

On the chin: *Just begin with one thing at a time.*

Collarbone: *I can even set some time limits.*

Underneath the armpit: *I'll just start with the first thing on my list for 30 minutes.*

Top of the head: *I can ground my energy and focus on one thing at a time.Yes, one thing at a time.*

Back to the karate-chop point: *I love and accept myself.*

I release my hands and I take a deep breath. I feel the water running down my back.

I'm ready to start my day with one thing and allow the rest to flow from here. Don't need the coffee, just the list.

You know, tapping is a great way to ground energy, reduce overwhelm, and be successful with your time.

CONFESSION #12

I Have the Mind
of a Monkey

I've been told many times that I am a natural speaker, yet I struggle with this. I can lead a group meditation or even a ceremony without any hesitation.

It doesn't matter how many people are in the group ... no problem.

But the minute I think of speaking ... fear arises.

What will I talk about? What will I say? Will they like my topic?

There really isn't much difference between speaking to a group or leading a group in meditation.

I mean I am still out front and on stage, but the topics are different.

Maybe I'm just too "out there" talking about the spirit within.

Maybe I'll look foolish.

But I know that speaking engagements will help me get the recognition I need. And I like to talk to people about this work, just like I like to lead the meditations.

But then there is that fear from yesterday and all the days before. They all come flooding in … *the weight* … *I'm no good* … *my self-worth* … all those limiting beliefs.

Why now? Why, when I'm finally making some headway?

My phone is ringing.

My schedule is filling up.

Yet I sit here in a panic to book these engagements because I am letting all this stuff cloud my head.

It's just the chatter of the mind … a monkey mind.

But it is so powerful! It's like there are two people within me. Me and this other person who keeps feeding my mind with thoughts.

I find myself spinning in a groove with the same thoughts … over and over.

It's not productive to my day. Especially when I've come so far toward really living my purpose and actually doing it.

Sure, there are days that can be tough, but I'm out there pushing ahead.

It's just the monkey mind.

It's the ego speaking.

It's the ego talking me out of everything I want to do.

I need to put the ego aside. I'll tell it to go take a coffee break. Isn't that what my teacher, Ted Robinson, used to say to help us calm the mind? My ego keeps getting in my way and clouding my thoughts.

Here I am, standing in the shower. My mind is so busy that I've forgotten to turn the water on.

At the karate-chop point: *Even though I allow my monkey mind to take over, I love and accept myself completely.*

Even though I allow my ego to jump in, I love and accept myself completely.

Even though I allow my monkey mind to get the best of me, I love and accept myself completely.

At the eyebrow point: *My ego gets the best of me.*

Side of the eye: *All these thoughts.*

Underneath the eye: *All these thoughts just get in my way.*

Underneath the nose: *I need to stop them.*

On the chin: *Tell the ego to take a break.*

Collarbone: *Take a break, ego. Take a break.*

Underneath the armpit: *I'll call you back later.*

Top of the head: *I need to be one-pointed in my focus.*

At the eyebrow point: *Bring my focus to that place between the eyebrows, the ajna.*

Side of the eye: *Yes, one-pointed focus.*

Underneath the eye: *All those random thoughts just get in my way.*

Underneath the nose: *Time to let this monkey mind rest.*

On the chin: *All these thoughts distract me.*

Collarbone: *It's just my ego.*

Underneath the armpit: *Time to take a break ego.*

Top of the head: *Take a deep breath.*

At the eyebrow point: *One-pointed focus.*

Side of the eye: *One-pointed focus.*

Underneath the eye: *One-pointed focus.*

Underneath the nose: *Back to my center.*

On the chin: *One-pointed focus.*

Collarbone: *I can pull my brain together.*

Underneath the armpit: *I can stop all this chitchat.*

Top of the head: *No more monkey mind.*

At the eyebrow point: *One-pointed focus.*

Side of the eye: *Focus.*

Underneath the eye: *I choose to release all these thoughts and remain one-pointed with my focus.*

Underneath the nose: *Time to let this monkey mind rest.*

On the chin: *One-pointed focus.*

Collarbone: *Focus.*

Underneath the armpit: *I can focus.*

Top of the head: *I am focused.*

Back to the karate-chop point: *I love and accept myself.*

I release my hands and I take a deep breath. I feel the water running down my back.

I get out of the shower feeling very centered and focused. I know what to speak about, so time to book those engagements!

CONFESSION #13

I'm So Depressed

O MG. I can't get out of bed today. I use Reiki energy on myself. I dream about my work, but I'm feeling so depressed.

It seems once again my phone isn't ringing for appointments. My studio is empty.

What is going on, Universe?

I thought I was over this phase.

Maybe all this work is going nowhere.

I'm back to thinking, *How can I help others when I can't help myself?*

I'm just going to hide today.

Stay in bed all day. No one will notice. No one is calling me, anyway.

I'll just sleep today and then I won't have to face that damn shower or me.

The tears cover my pillows. I don't know how I am going to face this day.

I'm glad it's still dark out. No one will see me crying in this bed of pillows.

No one will notice my struggles.

But I do.

I recognize that I am depressed. I've been working so hard, but for what? A day in bed is just what is needed.

Yes … rest is good for me. But … I've got to raise my vibration. I can't let my energy spiral down. It's too easy to get caught in this spiral. This downward pull can really take me down fast if I let it. So why don't I let it? Nothing is going to help me. I just want to give up.

Really, just give up?

Yeah, why not?

I'm no further than when I was that struggling kid out of college in New York City, wanting to be a dancer. I remember feeling depressed and alone in that big city. I gave up then. I might as well give up now. I'm depressed and alone in a small city. It's no different.

And I notice I'm not even in the shower … but I'm tapping on the karate-chop point at this moment.

At the karate-chop point: *Even though I just want to give up, I love and accept myself completely.*

Even though I just want to give up, I love and accept myself completely.

Even though I just want to give up, I love and accept myself completely.

Even though I just want to give up, I love and accept myself completely.

Even though I just want to give up, I love and accept myself completely.

Even though I just want to give up, I love and accept myself completely.

Wow, even this has the power to help me. Just tapping on the karate-chop point is moving some energy for me this morning.

I take a deep breath. I still notice the dullness in my spirit, yet I can feel the power of those words and the movement of energy within propelling me to my meditation cushion. But first ... a shower—actually, a bath today. A long soak with some Epsom salts.

As I sit in the tub, the thoughts begin to slow.

I allow them to come up as I half-heartedly begin to tap.

At the eyebrow point: *I just want to give up. It's just too hard.*

Side of the eye: *No it's not, Terri.*

I don't even think this tapping works.

Underneath the eye: *Yes it is. No it's not. I'll just give up. What does it matter anyway?*

Just keep tapping.

Underneath the nose: *It matters. It really matters. I have a gift to serve. I have a gift to help people make radical changes in their lives. What's so great about having these gifts, anyway? I'm depressed. Not getting anywhere.*

On the chin: *This gift is letting me down.*

Collarbone: *Did I really think it would be easy? Ah ...*

Underneath the armpit: *I can't fall into this depression. I can't let myself spiral down. Look for the lesson.*

Top of the head: *I can't give up ... now or ever. I can't give up ... now or ever. I won't ... I won't ... I won't.*

At the eyebrow point: *I just want to give up. It's just too hard.*

Side of the eye: *No it's not, Terri.*

Underneath the eye: *Yes it is. No it's not. I'll just give up. What does it matter, anyway?*

Underneath the nose: *We've been through this. It matters.*

On the chin: *It really matters. I have a gift to help people make radical changes in their lives. What's so great about having these gifts, anyway? I'm depressed. Not getting anywhere.*

Collarbone: *Did I really think it would be easy? Ah ...*

Underneath the armpit: *I can't fall into this depression. I can't let myself spiral down. Look for the lesson.*

Top of the head: *I can't give up ... now or ever.*

Back to the karate-chop point: *I love and accept myself.*

I release my hands and I take a deep breath.

I notice even without a lot of effort that tapping helps to raise my vibration, which helps to keep me from spiraling down and down into depression.

Depression is a downward-spiraling energy. It can pull you in fast, but tapping pulls you back up and begins to change the responsive behavior of the brain.

It can bring you from panic to peace in a matter of a few minutes. It shifts the energy and pulls you back up as you tap. It helps you to recognize and to release all those hideous thoughts and in many cases instantly feel much better.

CONFESSION #14

I Don't Know How I Will Pay the Bills

Monday … money … money … Monday … money … Monday … money money money … OMG!

Got to pay the bills.

It's the first of the week, first of the month.

Bills are due.

What am I going to do?

Why did I ever think I could live my purpose and make it?

Who agreed with me?

Why is this such a struggle?

I was doing OK at my day job.

I liked it.

Just wasn't the boss.

Just really wasn't my purpose.

But I had it made. I worked at home. Boss was not looking over me all the time. Lots of work to get done, but my day was pretty easy. And then I had to go and change it all … thinking I could make it on my own.

But here it is … bills due … AGAIN!

It happens every month.

And I'm still just setting up all my structures and laying my foundation.

When will my business start to pull in the dollars?

How am I going to manifest this money to pay my bills on time?

Good thing I don't pay the water around here … I need a shower.

At the karate-chop point: *Even though I don't know how I'm going to pay my bills this month, I love and accept myself completely.*

Even though I don't know where the money will come from this month, I love and accept myself completely.

Even though I just living on savings, I love and accept myself completely.

At the eyebrow point: *My savings is going to run out.*

Side of the eye: *My savings aren't going to last forever.*

Underneath the eye: *Then what?*

Underneath the nose: *Oh no … then what?*

On the chin: *I need income. I need income. But income isn't coming in.*

Collarbone: *I'm getting desperate. Why did I do this to myself? Who cares about living my purpose? I am so stupid. I've got to live.*

Underneath the armpit: *I've got to live. I've got to get a real job. Who have I been kidding?*

Top of the head: *Me! I've been kidding myself into thinking I can live my purpose and help others to live their purpose.*

Keep tapping, Terri ... Keep tapping, Terri.. Turn that water hotter! Let's really get this shiz out. Go through the rounds again. Let it all run out. Tap it out ... the water will wash it away.

At the eyebrow point: *My savings are going to run out.*

Side of the eye: *My savings aren't going to last forever.*

Underneath the eye: *Then what?*

Underneath the nose: *Oh no ... then what?*

On the chin: *I need income. I need income, but income isn't coming in.*

Collarbone: *I'm getting desperate. Why did I do this to myself? Who cares about living my purpose? I am so stupid. I've got to live.*

Underneath the armpit: *I've got to live. I've got to get a real job. Who have I been kidding?*

Top of the head: *NO, I haven't been kidding myself about living my purpose—just maybe about the swiftness with which I thought it would show up.*

At the eyebrow point: *I have to stay strong!*

Side of the eye: *I believe in my work and I know I can do this.*

Underneath the eye: *Go deeper, Terri.*

Underneath the nose: *This is what it takes to work with spirit and help others work with spirit … strength.*

On the chin: *Courage.*

Collarbone: *Faith.*

Underneath the armpit: *Self-love.*

Top of the head: *Self-love.*

At the eyebrow point: *I love myself and I love my work.*

Side of the eye: *Money is an energy. Money comes from source.*

Underneath the eye: *Just keep strong and open up those money channels.*

Underneath the nose: *No room for doubt.*

On the chin: *I pay my bills with gratitude.*

Collarbone: *I am grateful … I am grateful … I am grateful.*

Underneath the armpit: *I can pay my bills right now.*

Top of the head: *I can live my purpose.*

Back to the karate-chop point: *I love and accept myself.*

I release my hands and I take a deep breath.

I am ready to write my checks and pay all my bills with gratitude as I chuckle to myself and think, *Good thing my water bill is included in my rent!* I am grateful I can still laugh!

Gratitude is an ascending emotion. The more grateful I am for the money I already have to pay my bills, the more I can raise my vibration. A higher vibration helps to attract the very thing I am desiring. It connects me into a greater source, and that is exactly where money comes from ... from source. The universe is full of abundance. We just have to connect with that vibration.

As EFT taps away all those lower vibrations (thoughts of fear, doubt, etc.), it raises us back up so that we can easily and effectively connect with the higher vibrations of source.

CONFESSION #15

What If...?

L ive my purpose? What? Really!

What if my programs just don't sell?

What if no one signs up?

What then?

Admit to the world that I can't even live my purpose, and I'm supposed to be teaching others to do this? I've had webinars about it. I'm been standing on this platform for a while now.

OMG. If I can't sell it, then I will be worse off than before ... no job, no living, and no purpose. I've let everything else go.

The tears are just running today like a shower but from my face. I don't need to turn the shower on. My tears are wet enough.

At the karate-chop point: *Even though I have all these what-ifs, I love and accept myself completely.*

Even though I have all these what-ifs, I love and accept myself completely.

Even though I have all these what-ifs, I love and accept myself completely.

At the eyebrow point: *These what-ifs are keeping me up at night.*

Side of the eye: *These what-ifs are making my head spin.*

Underneath the eye: *What if these what-ifs are true?*

Underneath the nose: *But they aren't true, just my own chitchat of my mind.*

On the chin: *But they sure feel real.*

Collarbone: *What if no one signs up?*

Underneath the armpit: *What if my classes don't fill up?*

Top of the head: *But they will fill up … even if only one or two… that's a start.*

At the eyebrow point: *What if no one wants to pay me money or commit to working with me for nine months?*

Side of the eye: *That's the thought that kept me up all night! What if I'm not really who I think I am?*

Underneath the eye: *Yet the markings are there in my hands. Five gift markings … speaker, author, healer, psychic, radical transformer, according to palm analyst Baeth Davis.*

Underneath the nose: *These are my gifts, she says. These markings show me. I have confirmation right here in my hands … so why all these what-ifs?*

On the chin: *Stepping up to my life and removing all these what-ifs is all that is needed!*

Collarbone: *I know my hands are powerful. I know the energy they channel, and the lines are there to confirm this.*

Underneath the armpit: *I know the energy they channel.*

Top of the head: *Yes, there is doubt.*

It's 3:00 A.M., and I find myself tapping in my bed. Now I'm going to have to admit to being a bed tapper! Who cares? I've moved a little energy. I need some sleep. I need to just do a few more rounds.

At the karate-chop point: *Even though I have all these markings and I keep what-iffing myself, I love and accept myself completely.*

Even though I have all these markings and I keep what-iffing myself, I love and accept myself completely.

Even though I have all these markings and I keep what-iffing myself, I love and accept myself completely.

At the eyebrow point: *What if?*

Side of the eye: *What if?*

Underneath the eye: *What if?*

Underneath the nose: *It sounds so funny now ... what if what!?*

On the chin: *Just start with attracting one person, then the what-ifs will go away.*

Collarbone: *Yes ... one person ... the rest will fall into place.*

Underneath the armpit: *No more of the what-ifs.*

Top of the head: *Let it go and attract one person at a time.*

At the eyebrow point: *What if?*

Side of the eye: *What if?*

Underneath the eye: *What if?*

Underneath the nose: *What if ... nothing!*

On the chin: *No more what-ifs.*

Collarbone: *No more.*

Underneath the armpit: *Go with my decisions and let the rest go.*

Top of the head: *People will see the value ... it's never about the money.*

Back to the karate-chop point: *I love and accept myself.*

I release my hands and I take a deep breath.

I notice the peace that overcomes my body and my mind as I yawn.

I never realized I could tap to help me fall back asleep!

CONFESSION #16

My Work Is Stuck in My Computer

My writing. My photography. My art.

My landscapes … my Buddha shots … my tree images …

All my images are in a neat digital folder.

But I know I must I get them out of the digital form and into the art form that they represent so that I can sell them and stand up to that artist part of me!

I have a nice collection of Aspen trees that I shot out in the Wasatch Mountains.

I know that they can create a beautiful, sacred space, once hung.

I showed them via my iPad to a gallery owner, who loved them and offered me a show.

But I just can't get them printed and ready.

It's just such a challenge to get them out of the digital form and actually create the artwork.

All that *No one will like them* swims in my head.

It's a lot easier to talk about what I could do than to take the leap of faith and do it.

Print them out … hang them up … have an opening … stop!

Therein lies the pressure.

As an artist, many times I have witnessed myself doing some amazing photography only to forget I ever shot the photographs.

Yet my own healing studio has several hangings.

Safe … easy … I'm in control. Don't have to worry about selling them!

But isn't that true about all my work?

It doesn't really matter whether it's digital photos, books in doc format, jewelry on my beading table, speeches I write … it all needs to come out into the world if I am to truly live my passion in the healing arts.

At the karate-chop point: *Even though I can't seem to print my photos, I love and accept myself completely.*

Even though my work is stuck in my computer, I love and accept myself completely.

Even though art is stuck in my computer, I love and accept myself completely.

At the eyebrow point: *I know I need to print my photos.*

Side of the eye: *I just can't seem to do it. I'm afraid I'll make a mistake.*

Underneath the eye: *And no one will like them.*

Underneath the nose: *They have to be perfect.*

On the chin: *No, they don't. Just do the art!*

Collarbone: *Art doesn't have to please everyone.*

Underneath the armpit: *But what if I print them wrong?* And they come out wrong.

Top of the head: *But it's art.*

Eyebrow point: *That's where I need to focus.*

Side of the eye: *Just print one and go from there.*

Underneath the eye: *Yes, get the energy moving.*

Underneath the nose: *Get it out of the computer.*

On the chin: *Start with one print.*

Collarbone: *There is a pattern here. I've heard this before.*

Underneath the armpit: *And that's why I continue to tap.*

Top of the head: *Get it out of the computer.*

At the eyebrow point: *Do a mock-up. Plan it out.*

Side of the eye: *But it takes effort.*

Underneath the eye: *So what! Better than keeping them stuck in the computer.*

Underneath the nose: *But what will everyone think? That's the real reason, isn't it?*

On the chin: *And that it won't sell. And then I will have to face the gallery owners. And feel like a failure.*

Collarbone: *I'm a failure, and they won't sell ... they won't sell ... they won't sell.*

Underneath the armpit: *I don't know that. I won't know unless I try.*

Top of the head: *Just start printing.*

At the eyebrow point: *One image at a time.*

Side of the eye: *Be that artist.*

Underneath the eye: *Believe in the work, and the rest will follow.*

Underneath the nose: *Yes, everyone loves my studio.*

On the chin: *I can't be my only buyer.*

Collarbone: *I can sell them … no I can't … yes I can.*

Underneath the armpit: *They create a sacred space. Stay with this focus.*

Top of the head: *One image at a time.*

Eyebrow point: *I can do this.*

Underneath the eye: One print at a time.

Underneath the nose: That will build the collection.

On the chin: One print at a time.

Collarbone: *Just start. Commit to it.*

Underneath the armpit: *Commit to it.*

Top of the head: *Print them … print them … print them.*

Back to the karate-chop point: *I love and accept myself.*

I release my hands and I take a deep breath.

This pattern is a big one for me. It's one that I know will take many rounds of tapping.

I allow myself the space to grow and I create the time to tap it all out so I can be that artist for all to see, not just me.

CONFESSION #17

I Need to Get Visible

Some days we just need a little shaking.

We need a higher heat.

The issues feel so deep down inside, it takes everything we have to get it all out.

It's a Jacuzzi kind of day!

Sometimes we don't even know what it is. It's days like this when you just have to tap until it all starts breaking up.

I know I need to get out there in the world, but I don't know where to go.

I don't know what to do or which people to contact.

I just want to hide.

I want to fill up the Jacuzzi with bubble bath and hide beneath all the bubbles.

I know ... I can't put bubble bath in a Jacuzzi ... what a mess that would make!

So maybe I'll just stay in bed today.

Pull the covers up and declare another sick day.

Why not? I don't have to answer to anyone.

Except to myself.

I have to show up for me.

Even on days that I don't want to.

Showing up is half the battle.

One foot in front of the other ... step by step.

That's how it happens.

I know this, but my steps aren't happening today.

When I was just working a day job to get by, I could just come to work in any condition. It didn't matter if I was a little tired or a little grumpy. I could do my part, and then the bell would ring and my day would be over.

But now that I am working for me, it's a whole other story! I can't show up to talk to people if I am tired or angry. How will that help me to create business?

I know it's important to talk to groups, to increase my network of people, but I just get so damn shy.

People look at me and say, "What? You, shy?"

Yes, it does feel like that. Fear of that initial contact makes me shy to get out.

But if I never get out, how will people know me?

I recognize that once the ice is broken, it's not so bad. But it's breaking that ice that stands in my way.

I think it's like keeping the photos in my computer.

Just easier ... but not better.

If I am visible, then I really have to own all my beliefs.

And I can't make mistakes.

I have to be perfect.

Oh my ... into the water I go!

At the karate-chop point: *Even though I want to hide today, I love and accept myself completely.*

Even though I am having a hard time getting visible, I love and accept myself completely.

Even though I just don't want to show up today, I love and accept myself completely.

At the eyebrow point: *I just don't seem to want to get out there.*

Side of the eye: *I'm tired of showing up and doing all the work for nothing.*

Underneath the eye: *It's not for nothing.*

Underneath the nose: *It's my work ... my purpose.*

On the chin: *One step at a time.*

Collarbone: *Show up ... meet people ... do the work. So what if they don't like me?*

Underneath the armpit: *I can do this ... no I can't ... yes I can.*

Top of the head: *I can show up for me ... I can show up for my purpose ... I do have something to share.*

At the eyebrow point: *I just don't seem to know where to go.*

CONFESSIONS OF A SHOWER TAPPER

Side of the eye: *I need to get out there.*

Underneath the eye: *I want to speak and talk about this work.*

Underneath the nose: *It's my work ... my purpose.*

On the chin: *One step at a time.*

Collarbone: *Show up ... meet people ... do the work. So what if they don't like me?*

Underneath the armpit: *I can do this ... no I can't ... yes I can.*

Top of the head: *I can show up for me ... I can show up for my purpose ... I do have something to share.*

Back to the karate-chop point: *I love and accept myself.*

I release my hands and I take a deep breath.

As I get ready to step out of my bath, I realize I do like showing up for me, but part of my problem is I don't know where to go.

Sometimes issues are on top of each other, so we have to remove one to get to the other. As I realize the harder part for me is knowing where to go, I realize that this is what I need to tap on.

Being present and getting visible is actually part of the fun of having my business. I like meeting new people. It is where I get a lot of satisfaction in serving.

So I see the problem is that I just don't know where to go. Who to ask.

Who would want me? How do I find the people to reach?

Who can I attract?

So now that I know this, I know that I can't hide anymore.

It's time.

I'm ready for more adventure in my life.

I'm ready to get visible.

I need another round of tapping. I just touched the surface on this one, for this is the main issue, not knowing where to find my audience!

At the karate-chop point: *Although I don't know why or where or how, I love and accept myself completely.*

Even though I don't know where to go or who to ask for help, I love and accept myself completely.

Even though I just don't know, I love and accept myself completely.

At the eyebrow point: *I know I need to get out there more.*

Side of the eye: *I don't know where to go.*

Underneath the eye: *Or who to attract to my work.*

Underneath the nose: *I just don't know where the F to go.*

On the chin: *Why don't I know?*

On the collarbone: *I want to get visible.*

Underneath the armpit: *That's my word for this year … visible.*

Top of the head: *I must get visible … but where?*

Eyebrow point: *Who is going to want to hear what I have to say? I'm just different from everyone.*

Side of the eye: *Maybe it's not about finding but about attracting.*

Underneath the eye: *If I stay in a higher vibration, I can attract the people to me.*

Underneath the nose: *Yes, I can attract the people I need in my life.*

On the chin: *So what if I dress differently or think differently?*

Collarbone: *I can attract the people I need to contact.*

Underneath the armpit: *I can get visible.*

Top of the head: *I can get visible to get my work out there.*

At the eyebrow point: *I know I need to get out there more.*

Side of the eye: *I don't know who to call.*

Underneath the eye: *Where is "out there," anyway?*

Underneath the nose: *I just don't know where the F to go.*

On the chin: *Why don't I know?*

On the collarbone: *I want to get visible.*

Underneath the armpit: *Why am I even trying to live my purpose?*

Top of the head: *Why didn't I just stay where I was? It's too hard to get visible. I don't know where to go.*

Eyebrow point: *Why can't I just go anywhere? I don't have to always have a reason to get out.*

Side of the eye: *I can just get out.*

Underneath the eye: *Be visible.*

Underneath the nose: *Talk to people.*

On the chin: *Engage.*

Collarbone: *Just go.*

Underneath the armpit: *I have intuition.*

Top of the head: *I can just let my intuition guide me.*

At the eyebrow point: *I can tune into that.*

Side of the eye: *I can allow the energy to direct me.*

Underneath the eye: *And then I'll know.*

Underneath the nose: *Yes, I'll be guided where to go.*

On the chin: *I can get visible. I can be seen.*

On the collarbone: *I can attract.*

Underneath the armpit: *I can speak my purpose.*

Top of the head: *And live my spiritual path.*

Eyebrow point: *And help others to live theirs.*

Side of the eye: *Once I acknowledge it, I can attract it.*

Underneath the eye: *Like a magnet.*

Underneath the nose: *I can get visible and attract people to my work.*

On the chin: *I can help others by getting visible.*

Collarbone: *And then they can help others, too.*

Underneath the armpit: *I do know where to go … I am guided.*

Top of the head: *I do know … I do know … I do know. I am capable of getting visible to get my work out there.*

Back to the karate-chop point: *I love and accept myself.*

I release my hands and I take a deep breath.

Oh my, I am tapping and sweating it out! Stop the jets!

The more I get out there, the more I realize that this isn't so bad after all. I'm out talking to people about my work and now booking engagements!

Wow! So much unnecessary chatter of my own mind. It really is about quieting the mind, getting visible, following intuition, and allowing the spirit to be heard.

CONFESSION #18

I've Got Body Issues

Finally! I'm getting some response! I'm so glad I'm tapping all this out! I'm so grateful that I didn't give up. How could I help others if I gave up!?

Living my purpose may not be easy, but it is so rewarding! In helping others to make changes and connect with their spirit, it helps me grow stronger in mine!

I just received a call about speaking to a group about my program! The opportunity to reach even more people is so exciting for me! It's just what I was asking for. Right! I'm getting visible!

But I do have another confession to make ...

I think I need to lose a few pounds before I can get up on a stage and speak! I have to look perfect and be slimmer before I can actually get in front of a group of people.

What will they think of me if I'm a few pounds heavier? They will judge me right from the moment I step on that stage. I can just hear it now. *Look at her ... Look at that stomach ... She's got a muffin top on her! Who does she think she is? ... She's pretty, but if only she would lose a few!*

This weight issue is getting in the way!

I know that's what my problem is.

I'll lose 10 pounds, and everything will be perfect.

That's it.

Just lose the 10.

But the truth is, my confession goes deeper than that.

I'm not that heavy but I don't have a good body image. I notice how much it holds me back. I notice how much I shy away from being out front because of it.

This little secret of mine is really becoming a hindrance to my work.

I bet I could tap on it. I bet these tapping techniques could work on body image and weight issues, as well.

Jessica Ortner has written a whole book on it. In her book, *The Tapping Solution for Weight Loss and Body Image*, she teaches how tapping has a way of changing the response mechanism of the brain because it affects the amygdala, which helps us to change our behavior.

And that's what I need ... a change in my eating behaviors. And a change in the way I view my body.

All my life I have had a weight issues. Some years were better than others. I think this is where those issues arise from.

I was the only fat one in my family. I was the only one who always had to be on a diet. My older sister was petite. My brother was ... well, a boy. My younger sister was tall and very skinny. But I was average and fat and held on to these emotions.

But the interesting thing is when I look back on old pictures of me, I wasn't always fat. There were a few years when my weight was up, but it has stuck in my mind that I was always fat.

And now my perception of myself is so skewed. No matter what my weight is, I still feel insecure about it.

My emotions get the best of me and set me up to continue this cycle. And now I use food to cover them up. There's a cycle here that needs to break.

Like right now. I've been stuffing my face instead of dealing with these extra 10 pounds. I keep thinking food makes me feel better. Well, it does! But really it's a matter of how much food I eat. I eat healthy … just too much.

If only I could stop this behavior … and maybe I can with EFT.

But how can I get in the shower now? I have to get naked.

Once I lose these 10 pounds, everything will work out for me.

Once I lose these 10 pounds, I'll get the clients and book my programs and attract everything I am looking for.

So I'll just wait until I lose it to continue.

But that could be a while.

That could be forever!

Definitely not getting naked in the shower today.

OK, so I'll sit right here on the edge of the tub in my robe and just start.

At the karate-chop point: *Even though I feel 10 pounds overweight, I love and accept myself.*

Even though I feel uncomfortable with my body, I love and accept myself.

Even though I have a horrible body image of myself, I love and accept myself completely.

At the eyebrow point: *Maybe I need to lose just 5 pounds.*

Side of the eye: *Yep, need to lose 5 pounds, and then everything will be perfect for me.*

Underneath the eye: *Who am I kidding? This has nothing to do with how much I weigh.*

Underneath the nose: *It's not the about the weight.*

On the chin: *I am in shape. I work out. I do yoga. It's just an excuse ... fear hiding within.*

Collarbone: *It's an old thought.*

Underneath the armpit: *I can tap on lightening up.*

Top of the head: *Quit eating the chocolate. Quit eating the chocolate.*

At the eyebrow point: *Slow down and eat. Slow down and eat.*

Side of the eye: *Wow, it's overwhelm.*

Underneath the eye: *I just realized I eat as much as I am overwhelmed.*

Underneath the nose: *It's a similar energy*

On the chin: *Lots of overwhelm... lots of big bites.*

Collarbone: *This is huge!*

Underneath the armpit: *That's what makes me overeat.*

Top of the head: *I'm so overwhelmed I'll just stuff my face ... stuff my emotions.*

At the eyebrow point: *Separate the two. Eat for nutrition, not overwhelm.*

Side of the eye: *Eat for nutrition, not the emotions.*

Underneath the eye: *I can tap to calm down.*

Underneath the nose: *I can deal with the emotions.*

On the chin: *And let go of the old image.*

Collarbone: *I let go of the old image.*

Underneath the armpit: *I don't have to eat so fast or so much.*

Top of the head: *I can calm down.*

At the eyebrow point: *I'm not fat. My body is strong. I can fit into my clothes.*

Side of the eye: *I just need to slow down when I eat.*

Underneath the eye: *I recognize my emotions and then I can slow down and eat.*

Underneath the nose: *I let go of the old images.*

On the chin: *I can tap on all these emotions and then I can just eat my food in peace.*

Collarbone: *So what if I was fat as a kid? We all grow.*

Underneath the armpit: *So what if I was super-sensitive? It's a gift I have.*

Top of the head: *I can let go.*

At the eyebrow point: *I can be present with what I am feeling.*

Side of the eye: *I can be present to what I am eating.*

Underneath the eye: *I can be present.*

Underneath the nose: *It's not about the weight.*

On the chin: *It's about being present to what's going on inside.*

Collarbone: *I choose to let go of the old images and feelings.*

Underneath the armpit: *I am strong in my body. I am strong in my emotions. They are now separate.*

Top of the head: *I am strong in my presence to being in the now.*

Back to the karate-chop point: *I love and accept myself.*

I release my hands and I take a deep breath.

As I finish tapping, I recognize that it's an old body image of myself that I hold. With this tapping, I recognize that I can separate out my emotions from my diet and create a different response to how I view myself.

I also realize a very big part of this is overwhelm. This is a huge realization for me. EFT can control that overwhelm, which means that I can then control the overeating.

I am so relieved! It's taken me years to get to this realization!

I am OK with my body and my weight. It never hurts for me to lose a few, but it does hurt to use it as my excuse.

Let's book that speaking gig!

CONFESSION #19

I Don't Have Patience for My Life

I want it. And, I want it now!

There are many days that I question myself.

We all do this.

Right?

Days that I search the Internet for jobs.

Days that I wish I had just stayed right where I was … working my day job and living my purpose as a second job.

But I was only half-living my purpose but fully wishing I was an accomplished entrepreneur.

Today I look at my schedule, and basically it's okay but not that full.

Lots of busy work, a few new clients filtered in with the regular ones.

What was I thinking?

And then I think back to something I read in *Think and Grow Rich* by Napoleon Hill. It was about digging for gold. It talked about how close we can be to something yet not even know it. Right when we want to let it all go, the gold is just inches away. We may not see it, but it is so close.

I think of this every day that I get discouraged.

I need more patience.

How long has it been? A couple of months!

I turn the shower on this morning and allow the sound of the water to surround me.

I allow the bathroom to get all steamy and hot.

I step in and remind myself of the gold that is at my feet.

At the karate-chop point: *Even though I can't see all the results, I love and accept myself.*

Even though I am ready to give up, I love and accept myself.

Even though I have no patience, I love and accept myself.

At the eyebrow point: *Patience ... all I need is more patience.*

Side of the eye: *Patience with myself and the universe.*

Underneath the eye: *Remember the gold.*

Underneath the nose: *It's so close.*

On the chin: *No it's not ... it's never going to come.*

Collarbone: *My schedule seems empty.*

Underneath the armpit: *It's only one day, and you had a new client call yesterday.*

Top of the head: *Slow down ... it's happening.*

At the eyebrow point: *One day at a time... it's the F'ing journey!*

Side of the eye: *I need more patience.*

Underneath the eye: *I need to allow.*

Underneath the nose: *Be patient and allow.*

On the chin: *Trust the universe.*

Collarbone: *Trust the universe ... what? The universe isn't paying me ... but yes it is ... money comes from source.*

Underneath the armpit: *It's about the journey. I am living my purpose.*

Top of the head: *I can stay strong and have patience to let it all show up for me. I won't quit. I'll have patience and I won't quit. I quit all those other times ... trying to be an artist and not be in corporate America ... so why do the same thing again? Be patient and allow!*

Back to the karate-chop point: *I love and accept myself.*

I release my hands and I take a deep breath.

Every year I draw an Animal Oracle card for the year. The oracle cards offer reassurance and understanding. As I approach this new year, I draw the Ant card. The Ant totem show us that all good things come to us with time and patience. Ants work with diligence and conviction, despite their tiny size. They are immensely strong, with a great strength of will and accomplishment.

There is my confirmation of what I am tapping on ... patience.

Thank you, Universe!

CONFESSION #20

I Can't Seem to Finish My Work

Finally, I am gaining momentum in my work. The clients are booking. My events are filling up. I've got great ideas coming in ... but!

But I can't seem to see my projects all the way through.

Like writing this book.

I'm at the last few chapters, and it's just been sitting here waiting on me to finish.

It's as if I've lost the interest.

I know I haven't really lost interest but I'm at that point of finishing.

Finishing, for me, can be the hardest part.

Starting can be easy, but really seeing it all the way through ... hmm.

As a creative-type entrepreneur, my ideas are always flowing. Inspiration always seems to be coming in, but actually getting the work to materialize all the way through is a challenge for me.

I know this from jewelry making. You can't rush it. Finishing can be the most difficult part of the project. It can make or break the work.

I know this from photography. You can take lots of great photos, but actually printing and turning them into art pieces is another thing.

It doesn't matter if it is a piece of jewelry or an event or a book. The finishing of any project is crucial.

So here I am at that point with this book.

What is my problem?

Do I really want to get it out into the world?

What's the point of it, anyway?

Who's going to want to read it?

Time to start the shower!

I feel all the issues starting to surface.

At the karate-chop point: *Even though I just can't seem to finish anything, I love and accept myself.*

Even though I just can't seem to finish this book, I love and accept myself.

Even though I just can't seem to finish anything, I love and accept myself.

At the eyebrow: *Not good enough.*

Side of the eyes: *No one will want to read it.*

Underneath the eyes: *Can't let everyone see that I'm scared to live my purpose.*

Underneath the nose: *There are so many other books on this subject out there.*

On the chin: *Why is my book anything special?*

Collarbone: *What if no one buys it?*

Underneath the armpit: *Or reads it?*

Top of the head: *It will never sell …*

At the eyebrow point: *Just finish it.*

Side of the eye: *See it through and then get to the selling process.*

Underneath the eye: *Don't stop now. Finish it.*

Underneath the nose: *Quit judging it and just finish.*

On the chin: *Finish the book without attaching to the results.*

Collarbone: *I can do it.*

Underneath the armpit: *I can finish it.*

Top of the head: *I can show up for myself and finish it.*

Back to the karate-chop point: *I love and accept myself.*

I release my hands and I take a deep breath.

The calm returns. The water is clearing away this last bit of dirt. I feel the truth of this work surfacing.

Living your dreams is not usually the path of least resistance. It seems so much easier to hide and complain about life than to get out there and create the work you want.

As I have learned this past year, living my purpose is one of the more rewarding paths that I have taken. For years I have wanted to do work for myself full time. And now that I am, my first inclination is to go back to where I was. But as I use these skills of tapping, I uncover so much more about myself that propels me forward in a stronger and healthier version.

I know that I can help even more people because I, too, have lived many of these limiting beliefs.

I am becoming truer to my purpose as I uncover all these layers, which is strengthening my ability to tune into my spirit.

Tuning into the spirit and finding the passion within is where the purpose of life comes from. Once we can find this, we can apply it to any field or occupation in life.

Living from a place of authenticity is a key aspect of tuning into the spirit. And tapping all that other stuff out is how I have found that place.

Each and every day I acknowledge with gratitude the strength it has taken for me to get to this place. Sure, there are days I wonder why I am doing this, but the answer keeps coming back to my spirit.

CONFESSION #21

I Need to Commit

I believe that within each of us is a gift that wants to come forward.

I believe that gift can be found by reaching deep into the Spirit.

I believe that each one of us has the right to shine and to believe in those gifts.

All too often we go through life without looking within. We live on the surface. We fall into line with everyone else. We keep ourselves busy with the day-to-day stuff and wind up unhappy and complaining and blaming.

No, it may not be easy living our purpose, but it is rewarding and elevating.

It takes a commitment to oneself.

It takes a commitment to life.

In fact, that is a key component to manifesting dreams ... commitment.

Once you set your purpose, it is necessary to follow it up with a commitment, a ceremony perhaps that commits you to a time frame and holds you to your life.

When the going gets tough and you lose sight of that purpose, know and trust you can return to your shower of life at any time.

You can return to the chapters in this book to tap it out.

You can allow the water to catch your back and cleanse away the old and dirty energy that covers the enlightenment of your purpose.

Water does that for us.

It washes away the top layer of dirt.

It refreshes the body, the mind, and the spirit.

It offers us a ritual.

It leaves us clean and ready to go out and start our work.

Living your purpose requires it all. It takes a commitment to be courageous in the face of fear, doubt, and insecurity.

It takes commitment to hard work, but follows with a freedom of will.

It takes commitment to be strong to overcome things you never thought possible.

It takes commitment to living on the edge of life and taking that leap just about every day.

Shower tapping can remind you of that commitment. It can become a personal habit each and every day. Even when you are feeling good, a few rounds as you soap up is also beneficial to confirm your path for the day. Shower tapping can clean away the unnecessary or dirty energy that gets in your way.

So as we go through this final round of tapping, I offer to you right now—commit to your life and your spirit!

At the karate-chop point: *Even though it's hard to commit, I love and accept myself.*

Even though I know it's hard to commit, I love and accept myself.

Even though it's hard to commit, I love and accept myself completely.

At the eyebrow: *I commit and see it through.*

Side of the eyes: I *commit to living my purpose.*

Underneath the eyes: *But it's hard to commit.*

Underneath the nose: *I'm afraid to commit.*

On the chin: *I'll commit. I'll set a time frame.*

Collarbone: I *commit to stepping up to the plate each day.*

Underneath the armpit: *Wash away the fears and just tap.*

Top of the head: *One day at a time.*

At the eyebrow point: *I commit.*

Side of the eye: *I commit.*

Underneath the eye: *I won't give in. I commit.*

Underneath the nose: *I commit to my life.*

On the chin: *I am committed.*

Collarbone: *I know it's hard but I can commit.*

Underneath the armpit: *I can commit.*

Top of the head: *I can commit to showing up for myself each and every day.*

Back to the karate-chop point: *I love and accept myself.*

I release my hands and I take a deep breath.

I let the water wash all over me. The water hits the back of my body and I release all the excess tension and energy. I soap up one more time and let it all just drain away. I know tomorrow I will need another shower but for now, just for today, this very moment, I am committing to my life with all the integrity that I can bring forward.

I step out and into my life.

As Dr. Stephen Hawking says, "However difficult life may seem, there is always something you can do and succeed at."

I challenge you to find that something and bring it forward with the help of EFT!

To your spirit!

Epilogue

So what is my purpose?

My purpose is to live my life as a Spiritual Activist because I believe in the spirit.

I believe within each of us is a force fueling our passions and driving us to live our purpose.

I believe that force is our spirit.

When we can tap into our spirit, we can live our purpose any way we desire.

This is what I teach ... how to tap into the spirit.

As a spiritual development teacher, I teach the tools and techniques to help you find your spirit and tune into it each and every day. I teach the discipline and modalities necessary to build a spiritual toolbox that fits your needs.

Emotional Freedom Technique (EFT) is just one of the many techniques I offer, but one that is easy to assimilate into your life. It has many profound effects that can be achieved quite rapidly ... any time and any place ... like in your shower!

I've gone from being a single mom struggling to raise two kids in New York, working a full-time studio photography job with a side business of offering Reiki treatments, to now working full time as a female entrepreneur, owner of Natural Forces Studio, LLC, and the founder of the Spiritual Development Academy.

I've been trained in 10 modalities, have thousands of hours of practicum, and teach other gifted healers to build thriving businesses that help others tap into their spirit. I see clients privately, helping to mentor their own spiritual development and gain insight into their path, whether they are recovering from an illness, recently divorced, or just lost in life. I have been interviewed on ABC 33/40 and been published several times in *Reiki News Magazine*. I am the host of the Blog Talk Radio show, *Catch Your Spirit*. Each day I am grateful for all that I have learned by stepping out beyond my comfort zone and living my purpose.

For more information on spiritual development techniques, classes, and energy sessions, please visit my website at www.naturalforcesstudio.com.

And please follow me on:

www.facebook.com/terri.heiman
https://twitter.com/terriheiman
http://www.blogtalkradio.com/catchyourspirit

Appendix

The Practice of EFT

First determine what emotion is predominant (coming up) at the time. Look for emotions like fear, lack, self-doubt, overwhelm, or anger and set a SUDS (subjective understanding of distress scale) between 1 and 10 (10 indicates the highest stress). This is a subjective number. There are no right or wrong answers, so choose where you are at the moment. This helps us to gauge the effectiveness of the tapping. Simply use the first number that comes to mind. After each round, notice if that number has dropped and keep going through the rounds of tapping until you reach a 0, 1, or 2.

The Setup

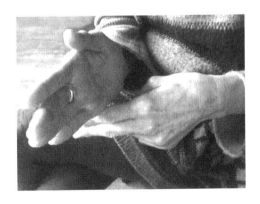

Start by taking the first two or three fingers from your dominant hand and begin tapping the karate-chop point continuously, saying something to the effect of, "Even though I have all this fear about living my purpose, I deeply and completely love and accept myself."

Repeat this three times.

By saying this we are doing a couple of very important things.

- We are acknowledging our emotions.
- We tell the subconscious mind that, although we have this emotion, we (the conscious mind) accept it.
- This offers relief to the subconscious mind that it is being validated by the more present self.

Once this setup phrase is repeated three times and the emotions start to surface, we move on to the sequence.

The phrasing of the sequence can be variations of the setup phrase or the story that runs around your head consuming your energy. It can be all those limiting beliefs or just one main belief. I invite you to use the words and guidance from the previous chapters. That's exactly why I have written them. We all share in these self-limiting beliefs. Feel free to add in any of your own words, especially the words that continue to run along the grooves in your brain.

It can be as simple as repeating one emotion ... *this fear* ... *this fear* ... *this fear*. The important part is to bring up the feelings, especially the negative feelings, that go with it. Really FEEL the emotions of the words you are using as you are tapping. This is what makes this modality so effective!

The Sequence (see diagram for exact points)

Tap about five to seven times with two or three fingers from your dominant hand.

On each point, repeat variations of our setup phrase.

It doesn't matter which side of the body you tap on. You can even tap on both sides at the same time.

Sometimes it's suggested to tap on one side with all the negative feelings and then end by switching sides, saying all the positive feelings.

START with the setup at the karate chop.

The points are: (see diagram)

1. At the eyebrow
2. Side of the eye
3. Under the eye
4. Under the nose
5. On the chin
6. Collarbone
7. Under the armpit
8. Top of the head

FINISH at the karate chop

Take a deep breath.

Release the hands.

Notice where you are on that scale of 1 to 10.

Repeat this complete sequence several times until you bring your SUDS level down as close to 1 as you can.

To see a video on this process go to:

www.naturalforcesstudio.com/confessions-of-a-shower-tapper/

Sometimes another emotion pops up, and you have to begin the rounds all over again.

This is quite common if you have a lot of deep-rooted issues.

Take your time. Notice how you are feeling.

Tap as often as you need, in the shower or out!

NOTIFICATION AND WAIVER

The information in this book is presented for information purposes and to share my journey. The material is in no way intended to replace professional help. In fact, I suggest that you seek out a professional EFT facilitator to help uncover the emotions as you begin to practice the technique.

Terri Ann Heiman and Natural Forces Studio, LLC, assume no liability for any client or third party for any damages or injury that may result from any treatment rendered in good faith from this book.

RESOURCES

I'd like to share the websites of my teachers who have helped me on this journey of learning and healing:

Gary Craig. http://www.emofree.com/
Ted Robinson. http://www.centerforinnerhealing.com/
Jessica & Nick Ortner. http://www.thetappingsolution.com/
Baeth Davis. http://www.yourpurpose.com/